crested geckos

understanding and caring for your pet

Written by

Lance Jepson MA VetMB CBiol MSB MRCVS

crested gecko

understanding and caring for your pet

Written by

Lance Jepson MA VetMB CBiol MSB MRCVS

Magnet & Steel Publishing

www.magnetandsteelpublishing.com

Printed and bound in Indonesia.

ISBN:
978-1-907337-16-1
1-907337-16-4

Contents

Introduction

The crested gecko (Rhacodactylus ciliatus) is known by several names, including the New Caledonian crested gecko, Guichenot's giant gecko and eyelash gecko. It is a reptile that has so much going for it, that it is no surprise it is so popular as a pet. Moderate in size, it is easy to feed and house and comes in a variety of colours.

History

History

Crested geckos originate from New Caledonia, a collection of islands found in the Pacific Ocean approximately 1,200 kilometres (746 miles) east of Australia and 1,500 kilometres (932 miles) northwest of New Zealand. Unlike many other island groups such as the Galapagos, they are not volcanic in origin. Instead they originally formed part of the continent Zealandia, which in turn formed part of the super-continent Gondwana. The lands we now know as New Caledonia then subsequently separated from Australia around 60–85 million years ago with the formation of the Coral and Tasman seas, and from Antarctica between 130 and 85 million years ago. New Caledonia and New Zealand remain as the two largest parts of Zealandia that are still above sea-level.

New Caledonia was named by the British explorer Captain Cook in 1744 because the rugged coastline of the main island Grand Terre reminded him of Scotland. In 1853 it became a French possession and now its political status is somewhere between independent country and part of the French Republic.

Fossil geckos are first recorded in Germany from the late Jurassic period (208 – 146 million years ago), long before the lands of New Caledonia were formed. Crested geckos themselves belong to the sub-family Diplodactylinae, which contains around fifteen genera including those found in New Caledonia – Bayvaria, Oedodera, Eurydactylodes, Dierogekko and Rhacodactylus. The Diplodactylinae are only found naturally in Australia, New Caledonia and New Zealand and these lands were originally joined into one – Gondwana – a fact that suggests that this family of geckos may not be island-hopping stowaways like so many island species, but that their ancestors have been there a long time - possibly since the dinosaurs.

In 2005 an additional New Caledonian gecko was described. Named as Oedodera marmorata , this gecko, or one very much like it, is thought to have been the original New Caledonian gecko from which all other gecko species evolved.

The crested gecko was originally described and named by the French naturalist Alphone Guichenot in 1866. He called it Correlophus ciliatus in a paper entitled *Notes On A New Species Of Lizard In The Gecko Family in the Paris Museum.*

The geckos he had access to were preserved specimens stored in the Paris Museum and were listed as originating from Noumea in the south-west of Grand Terre, and near Canala on its eastern coast. The crested gecko was later placed in the genus Rhacodactylus by George Albert Boulanger in 1883, who reduced the New Caledonian geckos then known from genera Correlophus, Ceratolophus and Chamæleonurus into the one genus, Rhacodactylus. The genus Rhacodactylus therefore contains five other closely related species, hence the crested gecko is now known scientifically as Rhacodactylus ciliatus.

Guichenot had described the crested gecko in 1866 from specimens collected, presumably, at some point after 1853 when the French had commandeered the islands. This gecko species then apparently disappeared from the face of the earth and was considered extinct.

In the early 1990s, with reptile keeping beginning to boom as a hobby, several expeditions were mounted to Grand Terre to try to track down this bizarre-looking gecko, but they all met with failure. In part this was due to Guichenot's preserved specimens and their listed source of origins – both from areas where we now know that crested geckos are not found! (It may be that Noumea and Canala are listed as the points of export and not, as was assumed, their locations of origin).

New Caledonia is prone to tropical storms and cyclones in the wet season. In 1994, following one such storm, a crested gecko was spotted on the Isle of Pines. Soon afterward Wilhelm Henkel and Robert Siepp visited the Isle of Pines where they discovered and collected some of the elusive crested geckos. This was followed by another expedition – this time by Phillipe de Vosjoli and Frank Fast, who also legally collected specimens in an attempt to establish the species in captivity. After a century, the crested gecko had been rediscovered.

Natural history

Natural history

New Caledonia has been designated one of the top ten biodiversity hotspots, along with such places as Madagascar and the Atlantic forests of Brazil. There is a high rate of endemism – in other words many of the plants and animals found there occur nowhere else in the world. With reptiles for example, some 60 of the 70 native species are found only on New Caledonia, and the crested gecko is one such. These endemic species are doubly fascinating because many of them reflect the ancient ecology of Gondwanaland that has been allowed to evolve in strict isolation from the rest of the world until relatively recently.

Crested geckos are inhabitants of the New Caledonian primary rainforest. They are semi-arboreal and are typically found in shrubs and small trees, spending much of the daylight hours curled in the branches and foliage of such vegetation. They are found in a few scattered rainforest localities in New Caledonia.

New Caledonia straddles the Tropic of Capricorn and has two main seasons: a dry season, and a wet season. The dry and cooler months are from April to November with daily temperature ranges from 17-27 °C. During the wet season, December to March, the temperature can reach 32 °C at midday. The high rainfall average plus warm temperatures produce a warm, humid atmosphere in the forests where crested geckos are naturally found.

Crested geckos are nocturnal and they will start to stir during the early evening. During the day they hide, either coiled in foliage or in cracks and crevices. Rarely are they found on the ground. At night they forage and mate. Wild diet consists of soft fruits, insects (and other invertebrates) plus the occasional smaller lizard.

There are few native potential predators of wild crested geckos. There are several native birds of prey, plus other avian predators such as the highly endangered kagu (Rhynochetos jubatus) but only the nocturnal New Caledonia Barn Owl (Tyto alba lulu) is likely to pose a serious threat. Other than that, the main threat to young crested geckos is likely to be other lizards, including adult cresteds!

Conservation

Conservation

Wild crested geckos are found in a very restricted habitat that is under threat. There whole surface area of the world where they are found is less than 500 km^2, and to make matters worse their rainforest habitats are becoming fragmented and altered by local agriculture and mining activities, especially for nickel. Introduced exotic pests such as rats and cats predate all life stages of this and other geckos. More sinister still are the introduced Little Fire Ants (Wasmannia auropunctata), native to Central and South America. These will kill hatchlings and attack adults as well as out-competing native invertebrate species.

Finally, following their rediscovery, a number of crested geckos were illegally taken or smuggled from New Caledonia to form breeding stock for hobbyists.

The crested gecko is not as yet IUCN listed by the International Union for the Conservation of Nature (IUCN), but is under consideration. Given their restricted base, high level of environmental threats and aspects of their biology, crested geckos appear to fulfill the requirements to be listed as vulnerable.

The crested
gecko

The crested gecko

Adult crested geckos measure around 10 to 12 cm (4-5 inches) SVL (snout-vent length – literally the linear distance between the most forward point of the snout and the cloacal slit) with tails another 8 to 10 cm (3-4 inches). Weights can be up to 65 g (2.3 oz) in large females. Lifespan is uncertain, some of those crested geckos collected in 1994 are still alive and so best estimates suggest they can live for around 20 years with good care.

Crested geckos have a typical lizard body plan of four legs and a tail. Adult cresties may lose their tail and should this happen it will not regrow, instead it will round off into a small, pointed stump, albeit at no obvious detriment to the gecko. The body of a healthy adult crested gecko appears quite chunky giving it an almost squat appearance.

Each foot has five toes; the tail is long and prehensile, able to partly wrap around branches and other perches and is aided by a patch of adhesive lamellae at the very tip (see later).

The head is comparatively large compared to the body and is triangular shaped, with the angle of the jaw extending back beyond the eye to give the gecko a wide gape. In the genus Rhacodactylus, the crested gecko actually has the smallest skull and body size yet the highest tooth count – some 177 although the continual tooth replacement that occurs means that small gaps in teeth may be seen. At the back of the mouth are the endolymphatic glands or sacs. If you encourage your crestie to gape, usually by gently tapping its mouth with a finger, you should see these right at the back of the mouth as two white bulging structures, These glands store calcium carbonate in the form of aragonite and are believed to act as calcium reservoirs, hence they are often more pronounced in adult females.

The skin is relatively loose and soft with small scales that give an almost velvety texture to the crested gecko. This slightly baggy skin allows 'wriggle-room' for some body rotation in tight crevice-like situations, and may help aerodynamically during free-fall after jumping.

There are skin folds along the hind limbs that stretch across to the side of the tail and these are extended when jumping, possibly to slow its fall. Crested geckos shed their skin as a normal part of their growth. This process is called ecdysis, and the skin is normally shed in sheets.

A healthy crestie will eat its own shed skin.

The most obvious feature of the crested gecko is the crest. This consists of a row of scale-like projections that start on the eyebrow of the gecko and extend backwards along the side of the head, the neck and then along the back before eventually petering out towards the base of the tail. In some geckos it will reach the tail base while in others it will taper off mid-way along the back. There are two crests – one on each side, where they also delineate certain areas of the body such as the dorsal surface of the head and separate the back from the flanks. This is interesting because these areas often carry different colours and patterns from the rest of the body.

The crest over the eyes is usually the most developed but there are efforts to develop cresties with elongated 'spikes' elsewhere along the crest, particularly on the head. These are sometimes known as crowned crested geckos.

The function of the crest is unknown – it may be a form of disruptive camouflage, effectively altering and blurring the outline of the gecko or it may serve in species recognition.

The feet of many geckos, including crested geckos, are one of their most impressive evolutionary adaptations, allowing them to walk not only up smooth vertical walls (although cresties have difficulty on clean glass) but also upside-down across ceilings. The underside of each foot is lined with ridges or lamellae, each of which carries thousands of keratinous hairs known as setae. Each seta is around 30-130 micrometres long and is only one-tenth the diameter of a human hair. It does not stop there however – each seta has hundreds of projections that end as 0.2-0.5 micrometre spatula-shaped structures. Attachment between the spatulae and the underlying surface appears to depend upon van der Waals forces, which are weak molecular attractive forces. Detailed measurements have revealed that a seta is ten times more effective at adhesion than predicted.

When walking upside down, geckos move alternate legs thereby maintaining the shearing forces that aid attachment of the setae. Discovery of the gecko's secret has triggered studies into the production of dry adhesives that mimic the 'stickiness' of the gecko foot.

The tail is quite long – often around the same length as the body. It is partly prehensile so that it can flex and either wrap around the gecko's perch or at least conform to the shape of it, both of which help with climbing stability.

The tip of the tail has a patch of lamellae like those found on the soles of the feet, giving further traction.

Crested geckos can shed their tail. This is a common anti-predation adaptation seen in many gecko and other lizard species. The tail detaches from the body, close to its base, where there are specific separation points in the tail vertebrae, the muscles and the blood vessels, so there is a minimum amount of blood loss and trauma to the gecko. This fracture plane is usually at the level of the sixth caudal (tail) vertebra. Once separated the tail muscles engage in erratic spasmodic movements for many minutes after detachment. This is highly attractive to predators and is used as a distraction to lure attention away from the gecko.

Pictured: Showing prehensile tail

Most lizards that have evolved this ability can regrow their tail given time, but for the crested gecko this is a once in a life-time event. The tail will not regrow but it will heal and skin over into a small stump. For a crested gecko tail-shedding is a last-ditch attempt to save its life, so should it happen the chances are that the gecko was very stressed indeed.

The eyes of a crested gecko are like beautiful orbs or gems set into the skull. In the daytime the pupil is a vertical slit but at night it widens to allow any available light on to the retina to help it see. Actually, the borders of the pupil are slightly crenelated to form small apertures that aid vision in partial light. The iris is typically a pale shade of brown with an intricate meshwork of blood vessels giving an almost marbled pattern to it. There are no eyelids; instead, the eye is protected by a spectacle or brille – a transparent scale which derives embryologically from the eyelids. Tears are produced and flow into the space between the spectacle and the cornea, keeping the eye lubricated and cleansed. Because crested geckos, unlike leopard geckos, lack any eyelids, the outer surface of the spectacle cannot be cleaned by blinking. To solve this problem cresties employ an ingenious and elegant solution - they use their moist and flexible tongue in a short sequence of wiping movements first on one eye, then the other.

Pet Expert | 39

Crested geckos have no external ears or pinnae, but they do have ears, which appear as slit-like holes towards the back of the head in line with the mouth. Cresties are nocturnal and can be quite vocal so it is likely that they have reasonably good hearing.

Crested geckos have three means of sensing food and other chemicals. These are olfaction (sense of smell) detected in the lining of the nose; gustation (taste) detected in the lining of the tongue and other oral surfaces; vomerolfaction detected in the lining of specialised vomeronasal organs situated in the roof of the mouth. Vomerolfaction picks up non-airborne scent particles from the tongue and lining of the mouth and may play a part not only in food detection but also individual recognition based on an individual's scent profile. This may apply as much to how your crested gecko recognises you, as it does to how it tells other geckos apart. Experimentally, a crested gecko responded more to the taste of banana or crickets than it did to lettuce or deionized water, suggesting that these (and other Rhacodactylus geckos) have evolved discriminatory taste ability alongside their omnivorous diet.

Reptiles excrete their metabolic waste nitrogen not as urea as we do, but as uric acid crystals – the white sand-like sludgy substance naturally present in their urine. This is not calcium, as many people believe. This is because reptiles attempt to save water; by excreting uric acid as a sludge they lose less water in urine than if they were eliminating it as urea, a substance that requires relatively large volumes of water in which to dissolve and carry it. The kidneys are paired structures situated close to the pelvis. Urine is formed here and is drained down the ureters (tubes that connect the kidneys to the bladder) where it is stored.

Unfortunately reptile kidneys cannot concentrate urine so this is further concentrated by having water absorbed from it across the bladder wall or by refluxing it back into the large intestine.

As with all reptiles, crested geckos do not have separate external orifices for the urino-genital tract and bowel; instead they have a cloaca which is a chamber into which the gut, bladder and reproductive tract all communicate. This intermingling of excreta is largely why crested geckos often produce urine and faeces at the same time The entrance to the cloaca is ventrally at the base of the tail and the entrance is marked by a slit-like opening. Slightly to each side there is spur called the cloacal spur.

Females possess two ovaries. Follicles form on the ovaries from which eggs are ultimately formed. At the stage of ovulation they just look like egg-yolks and are passed into the oviducts. Further down the oviducts a calcium-rich shell is laid down around the egg. Normally a clutch of two eggs, occasionally one in young females, is laid.

Male crested geckos have two testes that lie internally. They do not possess a true penis but instead have two structures called hemipenes.

These are found behind the cloaca at the base of the tail and in mature males two swellings known as the hemipenal bulges, mark their position. These bumps are not the testes as many owners believe. Only one hemipene is used at a time during mating, and it may occasionally be seen protruding immediately following a mating. This is nothing to worry about as usually it will retract on its own. The hemipenes play no part in urination. In front of the cloaca are the femoral pores. Look closely in an adult male and you will see a whole bunch of largish scales which appear to have a central dot – these are the femoral pores and they are relatively pronounced in sexually mature males compared with females. They are secondary sexual characteristics and, like beards in men, only develop properly after sexual maturity.

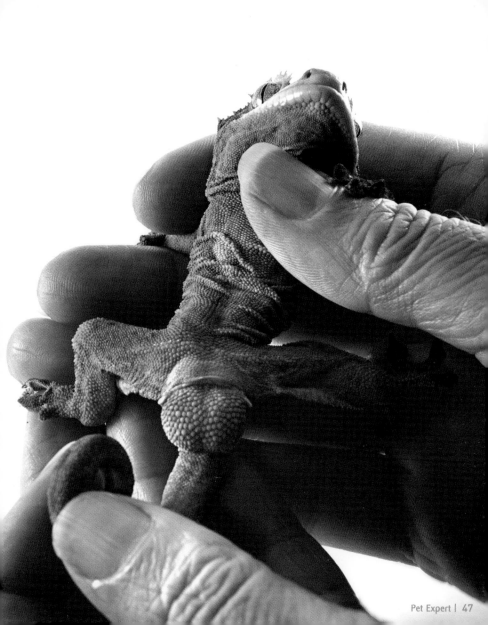

Crested geckos are ectotherms. This means that they do not generate their own body heat but instead rely upon external heat sources. They are nocturnal and therefore do not routinely bask in sunlight, although there is some anecdotal evidence from captive geckos that they will bask at dusk and dawn. It is highly likely that, like other nocturnal geckos, they allow their body temperature to fluctuate – sacrificing optimum physiological performance for the relative safety of hunting at night. During the day they may make use of warm hideaways, raising their body temperatures to aid digestion and other metabolic functions.

During the hours of darkness crested geckos are active lizards. When exploring (and this may be vertically up the side of your vivarium) they tend to walk with their belly close to the floor, unlike leopard geckos which are more upright. As they walk they tend to bend into a sideways curve, as if swimming, and move the diagonally opposite legs - for example, advancing the left fore and right hind simultaneously before swapping to the other two. In addition to climbing they are also fairly accomplished jumpers. When jumping they appear to propel themselves forward and upward by simultaneously straightening their legs and flinging their backs into an upward arch, both of which can give them momentum.

The toes are widespread and the skin fringes connecting the hind legs to the tail are extended to increase the amount of air-resistance to reduce the rate of descent. Its not particularly elegant or precise, but it works – so much so that, when handling your gecko, you should be careful; he may decide to take a leap into space without any obvious landing in site. Such leaps of faith will end with your gecko on the floor. He is unlikely to hurt himself, but he may escape behind furniture or be vulnerable to the house cat.

As a general rule crested geckos are not aggressive to other geckos or to their handlers, but there are exceptions. Adult males will fight and can cause significant bites on females during mating. Some geckos resent being handled and if unable to escape will attempt to bite. The bite is like a sharp pinch that rarely breaks the skin and is more of a shock to the handler (as indeed it is meant to be) than a potential serious injury. Hatchlings will often show reflex mouth gaping towards you when initially disturbed or handled.

Crested geckos can be quite vocal at night, especially when mating or when a new individual has been introduced into an established group. In such situations crested geckos utter a variety of small squeaks and barks. However, only they know what they are saying.

Crested gecko morphs – infinite variety

Crested gecko morphs — infinite variety

Crested geckos are hugely popular for many reasons but the two main ones are that they are relatively easy to care for and that they come in a huge variety of colours and patterns. The division of the range of types seen is useful from a descriptive point of view but in practice it can however be very difficult to pin down. There are two main reasons for this:

1. Different authors can have varying ways of cataloguing the variety of appearance seen in crested geckos and this can vary in its simplicity or complexity depending upon whether that author is a 'lumper' or a 'splitter'.

That is to say some appear to distinguish morphs on virtual minutiae, whilst others suggest more general categories and accept that there are gradations within that category.

2. Crested gecko colours vary with the time of day and their mood. The best colours are seen when the geckos 'fire up' – a term coined to describe the colouring when it is at its most vibrant and intense. This is usually at night when the geckos are foraging or mating and typically the colours become more intense and the patterning better delineated. It is argued that their appearance at this stage is what should define which morph they are.

There are three categories of distinguishing features that are used to describe a crested gecko morph. These are the colours, the pattern and any physical (structural) attributes.

Colours

The colouring of crested geckos is very varied and multiple colours can be found on a single gecko.

1. Red. Ranging from a bright red to a salmon colour.

2. Orange, varying from pale to bright orange.

3. Yellow, including mustard to true yellow.

4. Green, typically an olive green. It is thought that crested geckos do not have the necessary skin pigments to make a true green.

5. Brown, which includes tan (occasionally referred to as buckskin), fawn and chocolate – which is a very dark chocolatey brown when fired up.

6. Lavender. This is a pale grey-blue colour.

7. White or pale cream.

Patterns

The patterns here are distinct set of colour characteristics that are used to begin to describe the variety of crested geckos available. In reality, there are probably only four patterns – patternless, bicolour, flame and the tiger. The harlequin, for example, is really just a highly patterned flame, where the colour contrasts occur on to the body and legs, whilst the brindle is a tiger morph with a bar-code of smaller, less distinct stripes.

Patternless

The patternless really has no pattern – the clue is in the name! Patternless geckos are a solid or self colour and can be found in any of the above colours.

Pictured:
Patternless yellow

Bicolour

Bicolour geckos, as the name suggests, have two colours. One colour is found along the back between the crests, whilst the second colour is that of the flanks and legs. If this pattern is high contrast, the colour does not extend over the head and consists of several V-shaped patches, then it can be described as chevron. Those with non-V-shaped patches are probably just poor-quality chevrons.

Pictured: Bicolour

Flame

Occasionally known as fires, flame crested geckos
have a coloured pattern or dorsal stripe that extends
from the dorsal or crown of the head to the base of
the tail. It is similar to the bicolour except that the
dorsal stripe is of high contrast and may be split into
a distinct pattern. This colour is different and distinct
from that of the rest of the body.

Harlequin

This is in reality an exaggerated form of flame with
contrasting patterning not only in the dorsal area
but along the flanks and on the legs as well. Those
harlequins with an extreme amount of colouring/
patterning are now been known as extreme
harlequins! To be fair, a fired-up harlequin with
its colour heightened and contrasting is a real
sight to behold and these are often the most sought-
after geckos.

Pictured: Harlequin

Tiger (and brindle)

In this morph, reasonably defined stripes cross the body and run down the flanks to give a tiger-like striped patterning. The belly is usually a lighter colour and is patterned too. When this striping is made of many bands it is often described as brindle.

Pictured: Tiger

Traits

Traits in crested geckos morphs are distinctive characteristics that can be combined with the other patterns.

Pinstripe

Here the crests along the back are highlighted in a white or creamy colour and create a frame around the colours and patterns of the back. It is usually combined with harlequin or flame morphs but can potentially be seen on any other. Where the stripes are broken up they are called partial pinstripes.

Reverse pinstripe.

Reverse pinstripe is where there is a darker colour band, almost like shading, running beneath the dorsal crests. The result is two dark bands framing the back rather than white as in the normal pinstripe.

Pictured: Partial pinstripe

White fringe

The fringe refers to a white (or creamy yellow) line that runs along the back edge of the hind-legs. Sometimes a white patch appears on the knee as well and this is called, with no flash of originality, the white-knee trait. It is probably just a more extreme development of the white fringe.

Portholes/ lateral stripe

Some crested geckos have a row of white spots or patches running along the flanks, usually numbering around three or four. In some individuals these patches are more elongated dashes or even form a stripe, hence the term lateral stripe.

Blushing

When fired up these geckos have a reddish-pink flush to the under-jaw and throat.

Pictured: White fringed crested gecko

Dalmatian

The dalmatian trait peppers the gecko with black
spots. It is inherited independently, and when found
is superimposed on any patterns. The spots can
vary from small round black points to larger, more
substantial patches, and their numbers can vary
from a mild scattering to a marked blotched pattern.
The dalmatian trait appears to be dominant even if
only one parent has it then the young will also carry
the trait. Care should be taken when working with
this trait as it is so easily passed on into other lines
and may actually spoil the appearance of some of
the morphs. In some individuals the spots may be
red, or a combination of red and black.

Pictured: Dalmatian

Physical morphs

So far we have looked at colours and patterns – literally colour or chromatic morphs. But there are some physical aspects of the crest that are being selectively bred to produce structural morphs.

Crowned

Crowned geckos have extra-wide heads and the crests on the head are supported on fleshy flaps that flop down slightly.

Furred

Furred crested geckos have enlarged crest scales which give an almost furry appearance. These crests extend all the way to the tail base.

Pictured: Crowned

Designer morphs

Some particularly attractive combinations of colours and patterns have been selectively bred for and have been given their own names. These morphs are often referred to as designer morphs, a name that reflects as much their expense as it does their rarity. Three of the most sought-after are described below:

Creamsicle

Named after the frozen dessert of vanilla ice cream surrounded by orange-flavoured ice, these are orange flames. The orange body colour should be a bright, vibrant orange whilst the dorsal patterning should be a creamy colour.

Moonglow

These are patternless whites. Moonglow crested geckos should be as close to white as possible with no obvious markings. The colouring is very pale - as yet no albino or leucistic crested geckos have been produced.

Blondes

These are a dark brown flame where the brown should be a very dark chocolate – in fact as close to black as possible. The dorsal pattern should be a bright creamy colour.

Pictured: Blonde

Describing the crested gecko

Describing the crested gecko

If you want to describe a crested gecko then the accepted protocol for the order of description appears to be: trait/colour/pattern. Structural morphs are included under traits, so a red crested gecko with a tiger pattern would be a red tiger.

Similarly, a yellow crestie with a flame pattern and white fringes on its hind legs would be a white fringed yellow flame. Finally, a bright orange flame would be a creamsicle.

Always remember that beauty is in the eye of the beholder. The crested gecko is a beautiful lizard – a living work of art, whatever its colours, blotches and stripes. If colour morphs attract you most, fine, but the pleasure of having a crested gecko in your life is defined by so much more than which morph it happens to be.

Buying a
crested
gecko

Buying a crested gecko

Sources of crested geckos

Crested geckos deserve our very best care and part of that is preparing yourself for your new arrival. The first important step is to read about them. Learn what you can of their care and requirements, so that there are no surprises, financial or otherwise. Once you are certain that you can care for a crested gecko, one of the most exciting parts of crested geckos keeping awaits – purchasing your new companion.

There are several ways of obtaining a new crested gecko, each of which has its own pros and cons.

Pet store

This is the most obvious source of a new pet crested gecko, but there is a wide variation in the quality of geckos and the service that you receive. Pointers towards a good retailer are:

- The obvious health of the crested gecko (see later in this chapter). This can be difficult to judge, because crested geckos do not display well in shop vivaria. Inevitably they will hide behind vivarium furniture, or are scrunched up in one of the upper back corners. Their colour will be their subdued daytime attire.

- The provision of correct housing. This should be reasonably clean with minimal faecal soiling of the walls and cage furniture. There should be no overcrowding or mixing of species. There should however, be some climbing and hiding furniture such as branches and artificial plants. Remember that a shop vivarium set-up is different from yours at home – it is not expected that the gecko will live out its lifetime in the shop. The priorities are that it needs to be easy to clean and the gecko easily caught, so a more minimalist approach is often better.

- The store should have plenty of ancillary equipment available for purchase, including lights, vivaria, substrate and nutritional supplements. Books and other helpful literature should also be available.

- Knowledgeable staff.

If all of the boxes above are ticked its probably a good place to buy your gecko.

Internet

Purchasing a crested gecko via the Internet might seem attractive, especially as the prices are often lower than pet stores. You are, however, buying these crested geckos unseen – and are unable to determine the health of the gecko and their level of care – so there is a significant risk involved. Seriously ill crested geckos may been sold to unsuspecting buyers by a small number of unscrupulous suppliers, so beware. Run an internet search on the company you are considering buying from and check for comments, good or bad. Regulations govern the transport of all vertebrate animals, so your crested gecko should be shipped to you by an approved courier and not, as sometimes happens, via parcel post.

Private breeder

Buying from a private breeder should mean that you get an opportunity to assess the health of the crested gecko, as well as the chance to see its parents and the environment it was reared in. The quality of your crested gecko will depend upon that of the breeder.

Reptile rescue and welfare organisations

it may be that some reptile rescue organiations have unwanted crested geckos available for rehoming or sale. These will have been assessed by knowledgeable individuals and there will be a significant backup in terms of expertise.

Private sale

A significant number of crested geckos are bought from private homes or acquaintances. This is the riskiest means of acquiring a new crested gecko.

How to spot a healthy crested gecko

crested geckos are nocturnal so the chances are that when you go to buy yours he will be sleeping. He will appear relatively dull in colour and difficult to judge – a pale reflection on what he will be like during the hours of darkness The type of crestie will be more obvious – tigers, harlequin and flame patterning will be apparent.

Handling

Always ask to examine your crested gecko first, and either handle it yourself or, if you are worried about it jumping and escaping (or injuring itself), ask either someone competent to do so or view him in a clear container such as a plastic cricket carton, so that you can safely give him the once-over.

Crested geckos that have been handled well can be easily encouraged on to the hand. Keep your palm slightly cupped with the crestie's head pointed towards the top of your hand. This allows some control over the gecko and, should he decide to start wandering, place your other hand, palm upwards, in front of the gecko, so that he walks from your first hand on to the second. By constantly changing hands the gecko can move and explore without the risk of being constrained and panicking. If allowed to walk the gecko is also less likely to jump. Many geckos will 'taste' your skin with their tongue, using their vomerolfaction to gain more information about you. They may even learn to recognise you this way!

Some geckos are nervous or are not used to being handled and will object strongly if picked up. Typically, if restrained in the hand, such geckos will attempt to escape, firstly by attempting to run or jump.

If this fails then they may begin to swing their head and shoulders from side to side and as a last resort will attempt to bite. Their jaws are not strong, however, and a bite from a crested gecko is more likely to be a shock than cause any damage. Such cresties are also likely to defecate and urinate as well – possibly again as a 'surprise tactic' or maybe as a result of anxiety. Such geckos are best held in a more tightly-cupped hand with the head held between the outer edge of your index finger and thumb pressed lightly, but firmly, on to the widest point of the skull. The cupped fingers restrict the movement of the gecko, but do not grip or crush his body, as this can easily cause bruising and serious injury.

Give the gecko a general once over. Geckos, like most animals, are symmetrical, so any obvious deviation away from this should be investigated. Missing toes could be the result of bites from other geckos or from problems with skin shedding. Lumps and bumps are likely to be abscesses or possibly tumours. Kinked tails and curved spines may indicate metabolic bone disease. The absence of a tail is nothing to be concerned about other than for aesthetic reasons, providing the stump has healed over. A freshly-dropped tail suggests a recent stressful event or illness.

Gently tap the front of the mouth of the gecko and it is likely to gape, revealing the endolymph sacs at the back of the mouth where calcium is stored. These paired sacs should be obviously white.

Sexing is straight-forward in adults – look for the hemipenal bulges in males, just behind the cloaca, but hatchlings and immatures are difficult, even with the use of an ocular loupe.

Caring for your crested gecko

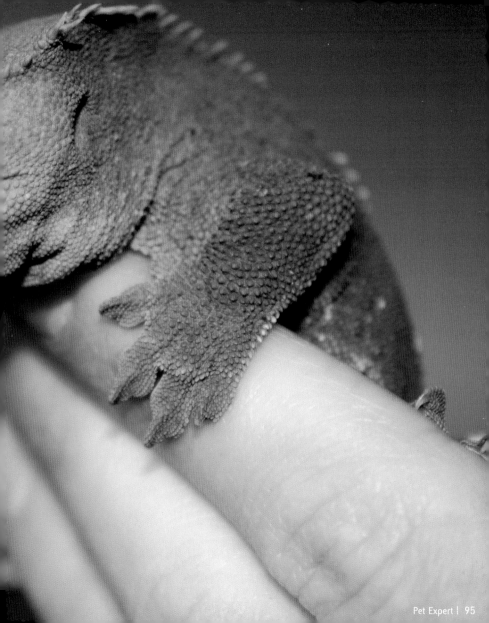

Caring for your crested gecko

The correct housing, possibly more than any other factor within our control, will govern how well we look after our crested geckos.

Previously, we have looked at some aspects of a crested gecko's natural history and how important parameters such as temperature and humidity are to these lizards. These vital needs must be addressed – a crested gecko will not 'adapt' to a life if these are not correct; instead, it will eventually become ill and die.

Many families have only one crested gecko. They are not particularly sociable and males are territorial, so keeping a lone creature will cause no hardship. However, the variety of colours available, their ease of breeding and the fact that they can be kept in groups means that many crestie owners soon end up with a collection of cresties! In view of that, here are some general recommendations on keeping groups of crested geckos together.

- Don't mix crested geckos with other species. Crested geckos have fairly specific environmental parameters and if these are not provided then they will eventually become unwell; there is also a risk of disease cross-contamination.

Crested geckos are carnivorous and will eat smaller lizards of any species. This rule can be relaxed if the vivarium is large enough, the other inhabitants need a similar environment and none are small enough to be consumed, but most of the vivaria available to hobbyists are not suitable for this.

- Keep one male only to a vivarium.

- Females and immatures can, in general, be kept in groups without too much aggression.

- Keep a minimum of two females to one male – more if you can. Some male crested geckos are over-amorous and this spreads out the attention of the male over several females.

- Hatchlings and young can be kept together, but watch out for bullying. Some individuals may eat most of the food, causing others to starve, plus twitching toes and tails may be accidentally mistaken for live prey.

Vivaria

Vivaria are enclosed, often rectangular, indoor housings that come in a variety of different materials and styles. For crested geckos height is important and a minimum of 45 cm is recommended, but the taller the better.

The simplest and least desirable of vivaria are those based on an aquarium or fish tank. Although easy to find, they have poor, top-only ventilation and access that makes them unsuitable. This can also make cleaning difficult.

Proper reptile vivaria are much better for captive crested geckos. They are made from many different substances including wood, MDF, plastics and glass. They can either be bought ready-made, as flat packs or even built by yourself from scratch. The potential size and scope of a vivarium is limited only by what you can afford.

Key features of a good vivarium are:

- Access is via lockable sliding or hinged doors at the front. This greatly simplifies routine maintenance.

- Water proofing. Crested geckos need a humid environment and this can lead to rotting wood unless the joints are silicone sealed. If doing this yourself, use a sealer designed for aquaria, not bathroom sealants that contain potentially toxic fungicides.

- Ventilation is crucial to the well-being of crested geckos. Normally ventilation is achieved by installing grids of mesh or plastic at opposite ends of the vivarium. These grids are usually positioned at different heights so that, as warm air rises, it exits from the higher ventilation panel while fresh air is drawn in from the lower. Some of the modern glass vivaria have mesh lids which, when combined with side-opening grills, greatly enhance airflow. There are also small fans available, which can either be connected to a timer, or better still to a thermostat, so that they are switched on when the temperature in the vivarium becomes too high.

- With glass vivaria, opaque strips may need to be placed along the bottom of the sides to provide a visual barrier that the crested gecko can perceive.

Perhaps the most difficult aspect of keeping crested geckos (and other reptiles) in vivaria is how to recreate the sun in the box. The sun provides crested geckos with both light and heat. Modern reptile accessories make this a great deal easier than it used to be, but it is still more convenient to separate lighting from heating, and this is reflected in the commercially available products. This separation of these two key elements allows independent control where necessary.

Temperature

In its simplest form heat can be provided by a spotlight or other tungsten or low wattage halogen bulbs that acts as a radiant heat source to mimic the sun. Ideally the bulb should be placed at one end of the vivarium so that a temperature gradient forms along the length of the vivarium to allow the crested gecko to select the temperature it prefers. These lights should be connected to a thermostat so that the vivarium does not overheat, and to a timer so that the light is not on for 24 hours a day, or worse still is perpetually flicking on and off as the thermostat reacts to the temperature.

To get around this second potential problem, there are ceramic bulbs available that only give out radiant heat. These are to be recommended because such bulbs can provide radiant heat throughout the day and night irrespective of the lighting regime. A less satisfactory alternative are red bulbs which produce heat and only visible red light, which is less disturbing to the crested geckos at night. Note that some people think that crested geckos cannot see the colour red – this is not true; crested geckos probably have good colour vision. There are also some blue bulbs available that emit light in the UVA spectrum.

Heat mats are also readily available and these are placed either under the vivarium or on the side to provide localised warm areas; they are, however, insufficient to warm a whole vivarium and should be considered as supplementary heating only. They can help to produce warm micro-climates under bark or similar.

Always make sure your crested gecko cannot directly touch the heat source, as burns can occur. The temperature beneath the basking light should be around 28 °C with a background temperature of around 20 to 25 °C. A night-time fall is to be recommended and temperatures down to 15 °C are tolerated, even by hatchlings.

Hot rocks – imitation rocks with a heating element inside them - should only be used with caution. Crested geckos will rest on warm surfaces, but if such 'hot rocks' are not thermostatically controlled then the risk of burning is increased. They are not strictly necessary and are probably best avoided.

Lighting

Crested geckos are nocturnal, and as such their requirement for ultraviolet light exposure is likely to be less than diurnal reptiles. Therefore, they can be kept successfully without ultraviolet if sufficient dietary vitamin D3 is provided – indeed if exposed to high levels of ultraviolet B light they will often turn a dark colour and hide away. They do, however, benefit from low levels of ultraviolet B and those bulbs that emit 2.0% ultraviolet B are suitable.

Artificial light for vivaria is usually provided by fluorescent tubing that has been tweaked to produce the important wavelengths of light for crested geckos, as well as produce a light that renders more natural colouring and so appears like normal sunlight. These fluorescent tubes emit light in the most important parts of the spectrum including UVB and UVA.

But there are some important points to remember with this kind of lighting:

Light intensity falls off inversely with distance from that light source, so that if one doubles the distance between the crested gecko and the light tube, the intensity of the light is halved. This is important, as suspending a full spectrum light several feet above a crested gecko will be of little use.

The ideal distance will usually be supplied by the manufacturer, but if in doubt suspend the tube around 30 to 45 cm above the spot where the gecko rests.

Many of these lights are rated according to their UVB output, and this is indicated by a figure at the end of the trade name. Typically these ratings are 2.0, 5.0, 8.0 and 10.0. Each figure refers to the percentage output of UVB and so a light rated as 2.0 should produce around 2% of its output as UVB. Crested geckos should have lights no more than 2.0.

The shape of the tube affects the area of exposure to suitable levels of ultraviolet light. The compact tubes (which resemble economy lightbulbs in appearance) produce a fairly narrow beam of ultraviolet light, while the longer cylindrical fluorescent tubes emit a more even beam over the length of the tube. Ideally the tubes should extend the full length of the vivarium, but if not, situate them close to the heat source so that your crested gecko will be exposed to the beneficial lighting as it basks. Mesh tops can filter out up to 50% of the UV-B radiation, however this is unlikely to be a major issue for crested geckos.

The lighting is best connected to a timer so that the crested gecko has a regular day/night pattern. I would suggest around 12 hours day to 12 hours night.

Always buy lights specifically designed for reptiles as many fluorescent tubes said to mimic the sun are colour rendered to deceive our eyes and do not emit the correct light spectrum. Unsuitable lights include those made for aquaria, general fluorescent tubes available from hardware stores and ultraviolet tubes marketed for inclusion in pond filters. These are especially dangerous as they emit UV-C and can cause serious eye damage. Glass filters out UV light and so the correct tubes are made from quartz – which makes them more expensive than ordinary fluorescent lights. Price therefore can be a rough guide to your purchase.

Unfortunately the UV output declines over time and these tubes do need replacing every eight to twelve months. Failure to do so may cause metabolic bone disease in crested geckos. In the past few years lighting that emits both the correct spectrum and heat have become available and work well. Combining the two obviously better mimics natural sunlight but it does take away some of the flexibility inherent in having both functions separate. Always provide your crested gecko with a hide of some sort so that it can retreat from the light should it want to.

Humidity, substrates and hygiene

Crested geckos are rainforest species and need a humidity of around 70 - 80 %. This can be achieved by a combination of several things, including regular spraying with tepid water, providing a moisture-retentive substrate and water bowls. More advanced vivaria can incorporate commercially available foggers which produce a fine mist. However, warm temperatures and high moisture levels can encourage a high environmental bacterial load, so hygiene considerations are important. Cleanliness therefore becomes a serious issue within the crestie vivarium, as it is in any relatively restricted enclosure. It is very tempting to try to set up naturalistic landscapes for cresties and they will benefit from it, but naturalistic vivaria are harder to keep clean because urine soaks readily into the substrate and faeces can be missed; there may even be a disincentive to remove soiled material in case it spoils the appearance.

There is no one ideal substrate for cresties, but because humidity is so important the substrate should be able to retain some moisture. Typical ones include coco coir, bark, orchid bark and vivarium mats or carpet, but try to avoid those substrates with moderately large pieces as these can be potentially accidentally ingested along with food.

Natural products (like bark chippings) if they are too moist, will harbour high levels of bacteria and fungi that can increase the risk of ill health so always remove faeces when they are seen, and replace all the substrate regularly.

Furniture

Furniture does not mean providing your crestie with a three–piece suite, just giving it things in its environment that it feel at home. It will need places to hide and structures to climb on. Hides can be provided as rocks, pieces of bark, empty plant pots, commercially available imitation 'dens', often made to look like rocks, plastic and acrylic plants (of which there are now some very good examples) and large pieces of wood.

Crested geckos are able to climb glass reasonably well and so make use of most of the boundaries of their environment. However, branches will help to increase their available exercise area, as will artificial vines and other structures. Adult geckos will leap from perch to perch, so ensure that any climbing apparatus is secure.

I also recommend a shedding box. The idea is to provide a safe place with high humidity where your crestie can shed its skin.

Commercially-made ones are available but a functional one can easily be made from a clean margarine tub. Cut a gecko-sized hole in the lid and fill the tub part with a moisture-retentive substrate such as vermiculite or coir. If they are breeding then an egg-laying box should be provided too, although in many cases a shedding container may double as a nesting area. And, of course, there should be a feed bowl and water bowl.

Naturalistic vivaria

Naturalistic vivaria – recreating a slice of New Caledonian rainforest – always seems like a good idea, but in practice is difficult to achieve. The principle is to create a living ecosystem with live plants and a bio-active substrate that will naturally break down faeces and urates. This can be achieved with care but the aesthetic result is not always good. For example, getting the correct light balance for live plants is difficult, but without it they will slowly deteriorate and die. A good way is to follow the example of the dart-frog hobbyists and use a false floor over a water reservoir. A thick layer of horticultural clay balls covers the base of the vivarium to form the reservoir, and is then covered by a porous sheet of plastic mesh or fleece. The normal substrate is added as the next layer. Water is added such that the level does not reach the overlying substrate, and is circulated up from the reservoir using a small circulation pump, the outflow of which can be used to create a small waterfall or other water feature. Water flows back through the substrate and into the reservoir. Humidity is kept high and the substrate is kept moist, aiding breakdown of waste material, which may be utilised by the live plants as fertiliser.

The down sides are that stocking densities should be kept low in such exhibits and high bacterial and fungal loads in the water will inevitably result from such systems, with a risk of parasite build up too.

Heating can be by traditional methods, although burning or desiccation of plant leaves may be an issue. Alternatively, thermostatically controlled heating cables can be laid into the soil.

Plants chosen should be relatively robust and would include Devil's Ivy or Porthos (Scindapsis), Sweetheart Vine (Philodendron scandens), Bird's Nest Fern (Asplenium), some orchids such as Phaelonopsis species, weeping fig (Ficus benjamima) creeping fig (Ficus pumila) and various bromeliads such as Neoregelia, Vriesea and Cryptanthus.

Electrical safety

Keeping crested geckos properly inevitably involves using electrical goods. Always use suitable products designed for keeping reptiles in accordance with the instructions supplied. If unsure consult a qualified electrician.

Caring routine

Good husbandry of any pet involves establishing a certain routine and I would recommend that you buy a small notebook to keep a record of what you do – small cheap diaries are ideal for this. When cleaning food containers and vivarium structures always use a commercial reptile-safe disinfectant, available from good pet shops. Never use household disinfectants such as bleach. Always keep your reptile-cleaning equipment separate from your normal household materials.

Daily Routine

- Check that temperature and humidity readings are in correct range.

- Refresh drinking water.

- Offer food in line with the feeding recommendations outlined in the *Nutrition* section.

- Spraying with a hand-held spray will help to maintain a high humidity and encourage your gecko to drink. If possible do this on a morning, in part to mimic morning dew but also to allow surfaces to dry and so avoid your lizard being exposed to a combination of cold and wet.

- Remove any obvious faeces as you see them.

- Change paper bedding if that is in use.

Weekly

- Thoroughly clean food and water containers.

- Clean glass doors.

- Search for and remove less obvious faecal material.

Monthly

- Thoroughly clean the inside of the vivarium making sure that you remove any faeces or urates from the sides and vivarium furniture.

- Weigh your gecko and log a record of its weight in your note book.

Six monthly to one year

- If you are using a full spectrum light, change it whether it appears fine or not (remember we humans cannot see ultraviolet light so we cannot tell if the bulbs are still emitting UV light just by looking). Make a note of the date in your diary or notebook.

Nutrition

Adult crested geckos are considered omnivores, eating both fruit and small animals, especially insects.

Proteins and carbohydrates (mostly sugars) are the most important sources of energy, with fats less so (but still necessary all the same). In practice crested gecko foods can be divided into three groups: insects, fruits and powdered diets.

Nutrient content of food

Food consists of a variety of different nutritional elements that need to be considered. These add up to the quality of any given food. Good quality food provides what your crested gecko requires while poor quality food is either deficient in some or all of these aspects, or else is inappropriate for the needs of the gecko.

Water

Water is an essential part of the nutritional content of food. In addition to feeding the correct foods and regular misting, clean, free-standing water should always be available.

Protein

Protein is needed for growth and repair of the body. In geckos it is likely that some is used as an energy source as well.

Fat

Fat, because of their insectivorous (and therefore carnivorous) ancestry, is utilized reasonably well by crested geckos. It is needed, especially by reproductively active females, as most of the egg yolk consists of fatty materials which are an ideal store of energy for the developing embryo. Because of this, the types of fat consumed by a female gecko may affect the viability of any eggs produced by her. Too high a fat diet can result in hepatic lipidosis.

Carbohydrates

Carbohydrates are also a main energy source for crested geckos. Primarily these are the simple sugars and starches produced by plants during photosynthesis. Fruits are relatively high in these.

Fibre

Fibre is important in two main ways. First of all, part of it is digested by gut bacteria which break it down to smaller molecules that can be absorbed and used by the gecko. Secondly, its presence promotes normal gut motility and stool formation, both of which are vital.

Vitamins

Just like us, crested geckos require a number of vitamins to remain healthy. Vitamins can broadly be divided into water-soluble and fat-soluble. The water soluble vitamins such as vitamin C and the B vitamin group, cannot generally be stored and so need to be manufactured and used as needed. Fat soluble vitamins on the other hand can be stored in the body's fat reserves. The most important fat soluble vitamin is vitamin D3. This is required to absorb calcium out of the gut and into the body. Without it, calcium cannot be taken up in significant quantities, even if a large amount is present in the food. It is produced in several stages. First of all previtamin D is converted to a second compound – provitamin D – in the skin under the presence of ultraviolet light.

Provitamin D is then further converted to vitamin D3 by a second reaction, but this is a temperature dependant change and so the gecko must be at its preferred body temperature for this to happen. Vitamin D3 is then further converted into more active substances in both the liver and kidneys.

Vitamin D3 is of animal origin and, when supplied as a dietary supplement, is considered to be the only form of vitamin D that crested geckos and other reptiles can utilise. This is important as many pet shop vitamin supplements contain vitamin D2 which is plant derived (and therefore cheaper) but will be of no use to the gecko.

Insects

A variety of insects are commercially available as live prey for pet reptiles. These include crickets, locusts, mealworms, silk worms, waxworms and phoenix worms. None of these insects are a complete diet in themselves and, with the possible exception of phoenix worms, are significantly calcium deficient.

Their main advantage is they move, which triggers predatory behaviour in your crestie. Some exercise is gained during the hunt, and they certainly contribute to environmental enrichment. However, crested geckos also take non-moving food items such as fruits and possibly nectar or pollen. So they can also be easily trained to accept dried insects such as commercially-available dried mealworms, dried crickets, canned crickets and so on – a fact that can make their management much easier.

Crickets

Crickets are readily available in a variety of sizes from micro (hatchlings) at 2-4 mm up to adults at 25-30 mm. Several species are available including brown (Aheta domestica), banded (Gryllodes sigillatus) and black crickets (Gryllus bimaculatus). Nutritionally they are pretty much the same, although bandeds have a slightly higher protein content (21% against around 15% for the other two). If crickets are not consumed quickly they can get hungry themselves and, on occasion, begin to feed on your gecko. Typically this occurs if too many crickets have been placed into the vivarium and the gecko cannot physically eat them all, or if the gecko is unwell and is not feeding. Always feed calcium supplemented crickets (see later). Crickets are also available in a dried and canned form.

Locusts

Usually the species is Schistocera gregaria. Only
the smaller locust nymphs (8 – 12 mm) are likely
to be suitable for crested geckos. These should be
dusted and/or gut-loaded (see page 135: Calcium
Supplements). As with crickets, be careful not to
feed too many at once.

Mealworms

Mealworms (Tenebrio molitor) are beetle larvae and are available in sizes from around 10 to 25 mm. Mealworms will not escape from a high-sided dish and can be kept there in a calcium-enriched powder until eaten. Some people have concerns about feeding mealworms to crested geckos as there are horror stories of mealworms chewing their way back out, once eaten. In reality this is extremely unlikely to happen in a healthy crested gecko – indeed their teeth appear to be eminently suitable for crushing hard-shelled prey. The adult beetles are unlikely to be eaten, and the giant mealworms (Zophobas morio) are not suitable for crested geckos. Mealworms are also readily available in dried form, often as wild-bird food. These are often readily taken by cresties and remove any concerns that feeding live may induce.

Waxworms

Waxworms (Galleria mellonella) are moth larvae (the adults are actually a pest species found in honey bee hives). They are quite fatty at up to 25%. Over-feeding may risk obesity in your crestie, but they are very useful in feeding egg-laying females which transfer significant amounts of fat into their eggs on a monthly basis.

They also contain the carotenoid pigments lutein and zeaxanthin. Waxworms can be fed at all stages of their life-cycle – pupae are eaten, as well as the adult moths.

Phoenix worms

These are the larvae of the black soldier fly Hermetia illucens. Lengths range from a mere 1.5 mm up to 20 mm. They have an excellent calcium to phosphorus ratio even without calcium supplementation.

Dubia roaches

These cockroaches (Blaptica dubia) are becoming increasingly available as live foods. They are relatively high in protein and on a practical note are not likely to develop into an embarrassing infestation should they escape.

Silkworms

These are the caterpillars of the silkmoth. Small to medium (up to 3 cm) are suitable.

Wild insects

Insects and other invertebrates collected from your garden or hedgerows can be used to vary your crested gecko's diet but please consider where they have come from.

You may not use insecticides in your garden but your neighbour might!

Fruit purees

Fruit purées are frequently used to feed crested geckos and are usually readily accepted. The easiest ones to use are those produced for human babies, typically for the age-range of 0 – 3 months old, and these are available at a wide range of supermarkets and other stores. Buy those which only have fruit and/or vegetables in them – do not use those with milk and milk products such as yoghurt, as crested geckos lack the enzyme lactase that is necessary to deal with the sugars in milk. Eating such foods could trigger diarrhoea.

On an 'as fed' basis many of these purées are low in protein and fat, typically less than 1% for each, and with around 10% carbohydrate, mostly as fruit sugars. Nutritional supplements such as calcium products can be mixed with them, as can the powdered crested gecko foods.

However, a common mistake is to offer crested gecko powdered diets mixed with purées as the whole or bulk of the gecko's diet. Consider that if you mix these 50:50 then the purée's low protein content dilutes that of the commercial diet's (typically 20%) protein, immediately halving it to around 10%. The same will happen with all of the ingredients.

Any fruit purée that is not used immediately can be decanted into an ice-cube mould and frozen, to be defrosted for later use.

Powdered diets

Commercially available crested gecko diets are available, and typically these are based on powdered ingredients that need to be reconstituted with water to a paste-like consistency before being offered to the gecko. Make sure you follow the reconstitution instructions as closely as you can. These diets have the advantages of being nutritionally more sound than insect-based ones, and they can avoid completely the use of live food. Crested geckos will eat these diets with varying degrees of gusto, and the growth rate of youngsters does not appear to be as rapid as on an insect-based ration.

Calcium supplements

Supplementing your crested gecko's diet with calcium is vitally important. Most of the food items offered to crested geckos are deficient in calcium (except good powdered crested gecko diets and phoenix worms). Remember that most of the commercially available insects commonly fed to lizards are not produced for their nutritional worth, but because they are easy to farm and they trigger normal feeding in insectivorous species.

Insects, because they have a chitinous exoskeleton rather than a calcified endoskeleton, are a very poor source of calcium and so this must be balanced with commercial calcium supplements. These are applied to the insects either by dusting a calcium-rich powder on to the prey, or feeding them first upon a calcium-rich food. This latter is known as gut-loading. Many of the commercial calcium supplements also contain vitamins, including vitamin D3, as well as amino acids. Young cresties which are rapidly growing, and reproductively active females, need calcium with every feed. Failure to provide this will eventually lead to metabolic bone disease (see Crested Gecko Health, Page 168).

Water

|Water

A shallow bowl, dish or water feature, containing clean water, should always be available. Crested geckos will also drink water droplets from a hand-spray or fogger.

Rules of feeding

- Clean drinking water should always be available.

- If feeding live food, offer it once or twice weekly. On other days have fortified purée or crested gecko diet available. Consumption of this can be intermittent – some days it will be ignored, other days it will disappear quickly and the dish licked clean.

- Never leave live crickets or locusts in the vivarium for longer than one day. Count them in, and count them out again (minus those that have been eaten, of course).

- The length of the largest cricket should be no greater than the width between the eyes of your gecko.

- Always clean out bowls containing fruit purées or powdered diets after 24 hours, as moulds and bacterial growth will spoil the food, attract fruit flies and potentially make your geckos ill.

- Geckos will happily survive for a week without feeding so should you go on a short holiday, feed them well for a week or two before you go, then leave them to it. Someone should check them on a regular basis however, in case of problems.

Reproduction

Reproduction

Sexual maturity in crested geckos, like all reptiles, is dependant upon them reaching a certain size and weight, rather than age. Therefore sexual maturity can be as soon as 5 months old if the geckos are well fed on a high insect diet, or as long as 12 months if slower growing on a commercial diet. Once a snout-vent length of around 7 to 8 cm is gained, hemipenal bulges will begin to develop in the males. As previously described, this is the most accurate way to sex sexually mature crested geckos. Adult females are often heavier than males and appear 'chunkier' with a thicker-set body. Females should weigh at least 30 g, preferably more, before being mated. Smaller males may be sexually mature but may not be physically able, or allowed, to mate with larger females.

Sexual behaviour

Female crested geckos will breed roughly every month for some eight or nine months of the year, resting for the remainder. This rest period is to be encouraged and has probably evolved to coincide with the cooler New Caledonian dry season. Dropping the temperature to around 20 – 23 °C should help to discourage mating, although many crested geckos will stop during the northern hemisphere winter period without the need to alter their environment.

Mating, as with most things in a crested gecko's life, occurs during the hours of darkness. It can be quite a noisy affair with both geckos vocalising as they leap around the vivarium. This may well be behaviour designed to test the fitness and suitability of the male to father the female's offspring. Crested geckos do not appear to form bonded pairings so a reproductively active female in the wild would be likely to have several suitors. Leading them on a chase should ensure that the strongest male is selected.

Actual copulation lasts for several minutes. The male will climb on to the back of the female, grasp her neck or shoulder tightly in his mouth whilst manoeuvring his pelvis to one side of her tail so that he can insert one or other of his hemipenes into her cloaca for a successful mating.

This biting can leave superficial wounds on the female and if necessary these can be cleaned with salt water or a dilute iodine solution. Occasionally after mating the hemipene of the male will not retract immediately. He will usually clean it himself with his tongue and it should retract within a few hours. If it does not then consult a veterinarian.

Egg production is quite a drain on a female's body resources. Fat is mobilised from stores such as the abdominal fat pads and carried to the ovaries, where it forms part of the yolk which has to nourish the developing embryo until after its post-hatching shed, when it can begin to feed. The shells of crested gecko eggs are quite calcified and this calcium, which is the last layer to be placed around the contents of the egg, is drawn directly from the skeleton of the mother and needs to be replenished from her food intake.

Practical breeding

Breeding crested geckos can be maintained in pairs or small groups of one male to 2 to 5 females. This can be in a normal vivarium or in a more clinical set-up with paper substrate and cardboard egg-carton material to provide multiple hiding and resting places.

Such set-ups have the advantage of being easy to clean and the geckos are encouraged to lay in an egg-laying box provided, making egg collection easy. These arrangements make it ideal for commercial breeders, but they are unsuitable for the home hobbyist who wants to give his geckos a more natural vivarium and the environmental enrichment that this entails.

In addition to the usual equipment and arrangements, a breeding vivarium should contain an egg-laying box and a ready source of calcium. The first can be constructed along the same lines as the shedding box described on page 110. Again, a clean margarine or other plastic tub (around 7 to 10 cm deep) is used and a hole is cut into the lid just large enough for the female to be able to access. Fill it to around half deep with a moisture retentive substrate such as vermiculite or coco coir and add just enough water to make it feel damp, but not soggy.

It is probably best to change this substrate after every clutch is laid, as some females will only use it once and will try to select another place (often beneath or next to it) to lay their next if it is not 'fresh'. A small dish containing a source of calcium, such as a commercially-available calcium carbonate powder, should be provided for the females. This is in addition to, and not instead of, normal calcium supplementation.

Preparation for breeding in crested geckos should begin during their reproductively dormant period. If you have the space, then males should be separated from the females but this is not a necessity. Make sure that the geckos are well fed and that plenty of calcium is supplied. Some breeders recommend checking the endolymphatic sacs at the back of the mouth as an indication of the gecko's calcium status. In healthy females these should be quite obvious, but a word of caution – I have seen prominent endolymphatic sacs in females suffering from metabolic bone disease, which may indicate that these individuals had problems mobilising their calcium stores.

Crested geckos lay a clutch of two eggs roughly every 28 to 30 days. Young females may only lay one egg for their first and even second attempt. There is no real parental care from either parent, although some females can be protective of the egg deposition site for a short while after laying. Pregnant females will therefore look to lay their eggs in a place they feel is suitable for the 65 to 120 plus days of incubation. They will chose a spot based upon the following criteria:

- Temperature. The female will want an incubation medium at a suitable temperature for incubation, typically around 23 – 26°C.

- Moisture. The embryo will absorb water from its surroundings as it grows; if the substrate is too dry then the egg and embryo will dehydrate; if too wet then the embryo may drown or bacterial and fungal infections could challenge the developing egg.

- The mother wants to feel that her eggs will avoid predation so she will choose a site with a reasonable depth of substrate, often in a confined space.

This is why egg-laying boxes are so useful. The lid with an entrance hole not only gives a feeling of security, it also helps to maintain a localised humid atmosphere and reduces the rate of substrate drying. If the temperature is correct and the substrate clean and damp enough, most females will choose to use them.

In females close to egg-laying, the eggs can, with practice, often be palpated in the body cavity as two firm pea-sized objects. This must be done very gently however as excessive pressure could rupture the eggs, which would trigger a massive internal reaction. If you can feel these then you know that the female is due to lay and you can keep a closer watch on her.

Occasionally in larger naturalistic vivaria, egg-laying will be missed or the egg-laying box will be ignored and the clutch deposited elsewhere. If conditions are right these eggs may incubate and hatch, giving you a very pleasant surprise when a hatchling is unexpectedly found. These should be removed as soon as seen because adult crested geckos can be cannibalistic to hatchlings.

Egg laying

Egg deposition occurs at night. The female will dig a suitable hole at her chosen spot with her hind legs. As she pushes the egg out, her back feet help to guide it into the hole she has made. Once both eggs are laid she will cover the eggs as best she can and will eventually leave them to their fate.

Incubation

Temperature-dependent sex determination

Whether temperature dependent sex determination (TDSD) occurs in crested geckos is still not known for certain. Many breeders want it to be true, but the evidence does not appear to support it.

In many geckos so far studied, sex determination of embryos is not dependent upon chromosomes as with mammals and birds, but appears to be due to the incubation temperature at a critical point of the developmental process. It seems that at given temperatures certain genes are either switched on or turned off and it is the proteins and enzymes triggered by these genes that eventually lead to the embryo being either male or female. It is still not known what benefit this is in nature, but in captivity it can be advantageous because, by altering the incubation temperature, we can skew the proportions of males to females to suit.

Practical incubation

Crested gecko eggs, unlike bird eggs, do not need to be turned so this makes making an incubator relatively straightforward. Commercial reptile incubators and incubator kits are available, but should you wish to make your own then any heat resistant container will do. You obviously need a heat source, which can be a small light bulb, a ceramic heater or a vivarium heat mat, connected to an accurate thermostat which, as a temperature probe, can be laid next to the eggs. An accurate thermometer is also required, and ideally a hygrometer to measure humidity should be used. These are available from specialist reptile outlets and garden centres. The incubator must not be permanently sealed, as some air exchange is necessary, even if this is only by lifting the lid once daily to check on the eggs.

The eggs do not need to be buried. Use a small container such as an old clean margarine tub and place some clean sand, earth or vermiculite as a substrate into this tub. Then place each egg into the substrate in such a way to create a shallow depression. The eggs should not be touching. Place a card or other label with the species and date of lay in the same tub.

Temperature is crucial for normal development, as is humidity. As a guide adjust the temperature to 23-25 °C and aim for a humidity of 70– 80%.

Incubation periods

the incubation length can vary considerably, depending upon the temperature of incubation (lower temperatures produce longer incubation times). At around 24– 25 °C incubation lasts around 60– 65 days while at the lower end of 20 °C it can be 120 to 140 days. Temperatures below 15 °C or above 30 °C are likely to cause embryonic death.

In some cases an egg within a clutch may exhibit diapause – a temporary halt in development, often at the early stages. This may be an adaptive process to stagger the hatching of young over a period of time, possibly to reduce the risk of exposing all of a given brood to unfavourable environmental conditions. Some pairs of eggs will hatch within a few hours of each other, others may be two weeks apart.

Apparent infertility

Adult crested geckos may be infertile for a variety of reasons, but sometimes their eggs do not develop because the nutrition of the adults is poor. It is wise to offer a varied diet with appropriate supplements as detailed in the nutrition chapter.

Failure to hatch/dead-in-shell

There are many reasons why gecko eggs do not hatch. In the first instance consider the following:

1. Temperature. Temperatures too high or too low can lead to embryonic death.

2. Humidity must be monitored and if possible a humidity of 70- 80% maintained. A very low humidity or a high airflow over the eggs can lead to an excessive loss of water from the eggs, leading to dehydration and embryonic death. An egg that loses 25% or more of its weight during incubation is unlikely to hatch.

3. Oxygen and carbon dioxide levels. Remember that a developing crested gecko inside the egg does breathe – not through its lungs, but across the egg shell. On the inside of the shell are membranes well supplied with blood vessels that pick up oxygen through microscopic holes in the shell and disperse carbon dioxide the same way. In sealed incubators or containers housed inside larger incubators, oxygen levels may fall and carbon dioxide levels rise to dangerous levels. Briefly opening such incubators once daily or every other day will prevent this from happening.

Once an egg is laid and has come to rest, the embryo (which at this stage consists of only an aggregate of cells), gradually migrates up to the highest point of the shell so that it eventually comes to sit on top of the yolk. After 24 to 48 hours it attaches to the inner cell membrane - the allantois. This membrane is important for oxygen uptake and carbon dioxide release, calcium absorption from the shell and storage of harmful waste products. This connection is essential but is, to start with, very fragile. Any rotation of the egg within the period of 24 hours after laying to around 20 days of incubation is liable to sheer off the embryo and cause its subsequent death.

When handling eggs always be careful not to rotate them. When removing eggs from natural egg sites to place into incubators always try to do it within 24 hours of laying and mark the top of each egg with a permanent marker pen or similar so that you always know which way is up.

Fertile eggs increase in size as the embryo develops and this can be one way of deciding whether your eggs are fertile or not. Another is by candling. This involves shining a very bright light through the egg. If there is a sizable embryo present it will be seen as a shadow and sometimes the blood vessels lining the inside of the shell can be picked up earlier in incubation.

However, often a shadow is not visible until almost the end of incubation – possibly because it is only by this point that the developing gecko is dense enough to block any light. Do not rotate the egg while handling it.

Hatching

As incubation progresses the shell becomes thinner in patches as calcium is absorbed from the outer calcified layer and incorporated into the developing hatchling. Eventually the gecko will hatch. There are two small "egg teeth" which it uses these to wear its way through the shell, creating a slit in the shell. Often, once the shell is punctured and a small slit made, the gecko will rest.

Eventually the hatchling will be able to climb out of the shell, a perfect miniature of the adult. Usually they are a reddy-brown, almost a light mahogany colour, but this will progressively change towards their adult colour as they age.

Occasionally some hatching geckos will appear to have trouble getting out of their shell. It is tempting to help them, but be careful.

The hatchlings often have large yolk sacs that have still not been absorbed, and the blood vessels lining the inside of the shell are still functional. It is very easy to damage these structures, with a serious risk of haemorrhage or wounding.

Rearing

These newly hatched crested geckos still have a yolk sac internally to supply them with food for the first few days and usually will not begin to feed until after their first post-hatching skin shed (at around three days old). Therefore at this stage you can offer them crested gecko diet and/or purees as discussed in Nutrition.

Hatchling cresties can spend their first few days in the incubator before being transferred to a vivarium. These babies will gape when handled in a threat display! It looks cute but remember, they think that you are a potential predator.

Ideally keep your newly-hatched crested gecko separate (or with its clutch-mate) in a small vivarium – the small acrylic pet carriers are ideal – until you are happy that it is eating. If offering small live foods like micro-crickets this will be obvious, but hatchlings do not make much of a dent in even a thumbnail amount of purée.

Once you see faeces then you know that your new gecko is eating and it can then be upgraded to a more natural home.

The husbandry advice discussed under Crested Gecko Care should be implemented, but of particular importance is the provision of hiding places. Hatchling and young crested geckos have many predators in the wild and so instinctively they appreciate cover, behaviour that will also lead them into appropriate micro-climates that help them to survive. This is especially the case if several babies are kept in the same vivarium. Humidity is also important, as crested gecko hatchlings are very susceptible to shedding problems and can easily lose toes from tourniquets of dried skin around their digits.

Selective breeding and genetics

Much of the interest in crested geckos is centred around the widely different colour morphs that are available, and because of this there is a great deal of interest in selective breeding to stabilise, reproduce and improve on these. Repeated close crossings can cause problems with reduced fertility and the inadvertent selection for bad characteristics, such as underlying heart disease (as is seen in some breeds of dogs). This risk of inbreeding depression could be worsened by the small founding gene pool of crested geckos brought into captivity (both legally and illegally). On the bright side many island endemic species appear to be relatively resistant to inbreeding depression. To minimise the risk always out-cross every two to three generations either with fresh stock, or keep two lines running alongside each other which you can occasionally exchange.

Finally a word on crested gecko genetics. As yet there are no clearly defined genes governing colours, patterns or structures in crested geckos. It would seem that all of traits identified as 'attractive' are under the control of multiple genes. Breeding like to like will increase the chance of reproducing or enhancing your chosen characteristic but crested gecko pairings will frequently produce young that are different from their parents and from each other.

One possible exception seems to be the dalmatian spotting which appears to act at least partly dominant, to the extent that if one or both parents have these spots then their young are very likely to carry them as well. Another is the white fringing along the hind legs. This confusing state of affairs may change should relatively common genetic disorders such as albinism appear. Typically these are simple recessives and may provide a practical gateway into the crested gecko genome.

Health

*Pictured: Gecko
which has recovered
from metabolic
bone disease*

Health

If kept and fed properly crested geckos are surprisingly trouble free. Many of the conditions that we do see in crested geckos can be traced back to poor management practices and therefore can, with some forethought, be avoided.

Crested geckos that are ill are probably best kept in hygienic-style vivaria where their environment can be controlled appropriately. Ideally use only newspaper on the bottom so that it can be cleaned out readily, and make sure that any vivarium furniture such as hides and branches can either be sterilized or thrown away. If your crested gecko is especially weak then remove any perches, as he may fall and injure himself. In addition to this the basic care for an unwell crested gecko should include the following:

- Provision of a stress-free environment.

- Provide an appropriate temperature of around 22 – 25°C. If kept at too low a temperature a gecko's immune system will not function correctly.

Also, if the gecko is on medication such as antibiotics, keeping it at its preferred body temperature will mean that its body manages and eliminates the drug in a manner predictable to your veterinary surgeon.

- Keeping the gecko well hydrated is essential. Many cresties will lick water gently applied to their mouths with a syringe or dropper. Spray the vivarium daily to maintain humidity and create further drinking opportunities.

- If you have concerns it is best to arrange a consultation with your veterinarian so that your crestie can be examined and its problems analysed and dealt with professionally.

Metabolic bone disease

Bone diseases can be common in lizards of all species, and any limb swelling, fracture or paralysis should be considered as a possible sign of an underlying bone disorder. Metabolic Bone Disease (MBD) is actually a group of skeletal disorders that are largely – but not exclusively - dietary related. Common causes include a dietary calcium deficiency, a dietary calcium/phosphorus imbalance, a dietary vitamin D3 deficiency, lack of exposure to ultra violet light, dietary protein deficiency or excess and liver, kidney or intestinal disease.

Signs of MBD in crested geckos include weakness, loss of appetite, swollen limbs and kinking of the tail. Closer examination may reveal that the jaws are extremely soft and can be easily deformed (please test this gently as it likely to be painful for the gecko). Excessive handling may trigger autotomy. The endolymphatic sacs at the back of the mouth may appear shrunken in size, although I have found this not to be a consistent sign. In females, eggs may be palpable in the body cavity and indeed this may be the final straw. Female geckos that have marginal calcium levels may go into a sudden calcium crash by mobilizing what little calcium they do have into their egg shells prior to laying.

Most skeletal problems in crested geckos are dietary linked and should a gecko start to manifest such signs then one should immediately consider the following:

1. **Diet**: Reassess the possible protein, fibre and mineral content of the diet. Consider increasing or improving the calcium content of the diet. Common mistakes include failing to supplement the food with calcium or reducing the calcium content of commercial diets by mixing with fruit purees (see the Nutrition chapter).

2. **Lighting**: Make sure there is provision for ultraviolet lighting. Crested geckos can be kept without full spectrum lighting but to compensate they must have dietary vitamin D3, usually combined with good calcium supplement. A daytime full spectrum bulb with a 2% ultraviolet output can be beneficial, allowing the gecko to bask if it wants to. Always check that the light positioning is appropriate (usually around 30 cm above the animal) close to a heat source (to encourage basking) and that they are changed regularly (every eight to twelve months). Ultraviolet outputs greater than 2% are unnecessary and will probably just result in your gecko turning very dark and hiding away.

3. **Temperature**: Encourage a temperature drop at night if the gecko seems otherwise well.

If the gecko shows severe signs or is lethargic or anorexic then seek veterinary advice, as secondary infections are common in such animals. Your crestie may need radiography, blood tests or other tests to establish what is causing the problem. Treatments can include injecting vitamin D3, injecting calcium, and dealing with other underlying causes, such as liver disease.

As a word of caution I have seen some cases of MBD which had well-provisioned endolymphatic sacs. These individuals had pronounced spinal deformities and tail kinking, which suggested some form of MBD. Such cases may be the result of an abnormal physiology rather than of dietary origin.

Floppy tail

This is a condition seen in crested geckos and some other gecko species too, especially the Madagascan day geckos (Phelsuma species). Typically this is seen when the geckos are on vertical surfaces with their head pointing downwards. The tail is not held against the substrate as it should be, but instead flops forward and to one side so that it hangs partly over the gecko's back. This condition is often linked with abnormalities of the pelvic bones (which is where some of the major tail muscles have their points of origin). It is believed to be the result of geckos spending excessive amounts of time in a head-down position on smooth, vertical surfaces such as glass. Unable to grip or conform easily, it may be that the strong muscles at the base of the tail become fatigued, allowing the tail to come away from the underlying surface. Eventually gravity pulls the tail downwards and in a gecko whose skeleton is still developing this abnormal loading of the pelvis will cause deformations of those bones, compounding the problem. MBD may also play a part in some, but not all, individuals. This problem cannot be cured but can be avoided, or at least managed, by providing plenty of more normal positioned rests, with due regard to stocking densities so that some individuals are not forced to spend prolonged times on the sides of the vivarium.

Parasites

Parasites are quite uncommon in crested geckos, although they are occasionally encountered.
This situation may change as crested geckos are progressively exposed to a wide variety of parasites from other reptiles they encounter in the pet trade and in hobbyist collections.

Coccidiosis

This single-celled protozoan parasite Isospora sykorai has been described in the crested gecko (Modr et al 2004), whilst another - I. leachiani - was found in the related Rhacodactylus leachianus. This does not seem to be common and the potential for harm is unknown – the geckos in which these were found appeared to be in good health.

Oxyurids nematodes

Oxyurid nematodes are small intestinal worms that are common in pet lizards but rarely cause serious problems. You are unlikely to see any worms in the faeces – their presence is usually given away by spotting their eggs on microscopic examination of droppings. They do compete with the gecko for the food that it eats and heavy burdens may cause weight loss, whilst lighter infestations may have more subtle effects, such as poorer growth rate and fertility.

The life cycle of oxyurids is direct and control is by worming with appropriate wormers, such as fenbendazole, available from your veterinarian, and by regular removal of faeces.

Mites

Parasitic neotrombiculid chiggers (mites) have been described on wild gargoyle geckos (Rhacodactylus auriculatus) (Bauer et al 1990) and it would seem likely that crested geckos would also be affected. In captivity occasionally the lizard mite Hirstiella (or similar) is encountered. These are large reddish-coloured mites that can usually be found in the skin folds around the various limb joints. Treatment can be by the application of topical fipronil spray once weekly for at least four weeks. This is best first applied to a cloth and rubbed over the entire surface of the lizard. Fipronil can also be used to treat the environment.

Abnormal skin shedding

Normal skin shedding is properly termed ecdysis – abnormal or problematic shedding is called dysecdysis. This can appear as patches of dull, thickened skin that may indicate areas where several layers of skin have built up over successive dysecdysis episodes. Rings of unshed skin may form bands around the tips of extremities such as toes and tail tips.

These may constrict as they dry, acting as tourniquets and compromising blood flow to the extremities. Crested geckos that have had previous problems may lack one or more digits. Such bands of tight skin need to be removed. Moisten the affected areas with a damp cotton bud in order to loosen the retained skin from the underlying epidermis. Retained spectacular scales in geckos can also be gently lifted and removed using a damp cotton bud. In crested geckos dysecdysis is commonly associated with low humidity levels and is especially a problem with hatchlings and young geckos.

Egg-binding

Any adult female crested gecko that shows non-specific signs of ill health, restlessness or persistent straining should be assessed for egg-binding (dystocia). There are two forms:

1. Pre Ovulatory Ovarian Stasis. The eggs grow in the ovaries but are not ovulated, so the ovaries become overloaded with retained yolks. This appears to be rare in crested geckos.

2. Post-ovulatory. Here eggs that are shelled to varying degrees are present within the oviducts. It is easily diagnosed by radiography as the shells show up easily. There are many possible causes for this, including environmental (no provision of suitable egg deposition sites), low calcium levels, fractured or deformed pelvis, internal tumours and so on, so your veterinarian may need to do several tests.

Treatment involves providing the correct environment, including appropriate temperature, humidity and nesting chamber, and this may induce normal egg-laying. Supplement well with calcium. If this fails then you will need to take your gecko to a veterinarian who may consider medical induction with calcium and oxytocin, percutaneous ovocentesis (where the egg contents are sucked out by syringe through a needle inserted through the body wall so that the shrunken eggs can be passed – this must be done under general anaesthesia) or surgical removal (a caesarian).

Finally some general points on salmonellosis in reptiles. These bacteria are probably best considered as a normal constituent of lizard cloacal/gut microflora. They are rarely pathogenic to lizards but excretion is likely to increase during times of stress In reality the risk is minimal to healthy hobbyists and infections in reptile owners are very rare. If isolated, treatment is usually not appropriate as it is unlikely to be effective long-term and may encourage antibiotic resistance.

Recommendations for prevention of salmonellosis from captive reptiles issued by the Centre for Disease Control in the USA are:

- Pregnant women, children less than five years of age and persons with impaired immune system function (e.g. AIDS) should not have contact with reptiles.

- Because of the risk if becoming infected with Salmonella from a reptile, even without direct contact, households with pregnant women, children under five years of age or persons with impaired immune system function should not keep reptiles. Reptiles are not appropriate pets for childcare centres.

- All persons should wash hands with soap immediately after any contact with a reptile or reptile cage.

- Reptiles should be kept out of food preparation areas such as kitchens.

- Kitchen sinks should not be used to wash food or water bowls, cages or vivaria used for reptiles, or to bath reptiles. Any sink used for these purposes should be disinfected after use.

References

Modrý, D. JirkĐ, M. and Veselý. M. (2004). Two new species of Isospora (Apicomplexa: Eimeriidae) from geckoes of the genus Rhacodactylus (Sauria: Gekkonidae) endemic to New Caledonia. Folia Parasitologica 51: 283–286.

Bauer, A.M., Russel A.P., and Dollahon N.R. (1990) Skin folds in the gekkonid lizard genus Rhacodactylus: a natural test of the damage limitation hypothesis of mite pocket function. Can. J. Zool. 68: 1196—1201.

Weights & measures

If you prefer your units in pounds and inches, you can use this conversion chart:

Length in inches	Length in cm	Temperature in °C	Temperature in °F
1	2.5	10	50
2	5.1	15	59
3	7.6	20	68
4	10.2	25	77
5	12.7	30	86
8	20.3	35	95
10	25.4	40	104
15	38.1	45	113

Measurements rounded to 1 decimal place.